Memory Mastery

35 Activities to Improve Memory and Brain Functioning

Creative Works

Table of Contents

Introduction

What was the last thing you had trouble remembering? What is a memory you have from long ago that you can still easily recall?

It's funny how the brain works. Sometimes small things stay stored in our brain our entire lives. In other moments, we might forget important dates and names of our loved ones.

The brain is the central organ of the body and one that can often be overlooked. We're told all of our lives to eat healthy and exercise to protect our hearts. We're taught that smoking is bad for your lungs and drinking alcohol is bad for your liver.

For many, we aren't taught to take action to protect our brains until we're already experiencing signs of cognitive decline. Humans only have one brain, mind, and subconscious. It's important to take the necessary steps to protect and strengthen neurological functions now before it is too late.

What the Research Says

The brain and spinal cords are among some of the few organs that we still have yet to have the ability to transplant. This means that our brains are unique to us and will be the only ones we will ever have! While there is still so much left to learn about the brain, researchers are working hard to figure out what they can do in order to help this vital organ thrive.

Potential Causes

What are the potential causes of memory loss? From diet to genetics, there are many different causes of cognitive decline, with the following the most notable ("Memory Loss," 2022):

- diseases like Alzheimer's or dementia

- certain medications

- sleep apnea

- thyroid related issues

- vitamin deficiencies

- mental illness like anxiety or depression

- head injuries

- alcoholism or substance abuse

There is even some research that suggests the suppression of emotions can increase your risk of cognitive decline ("Memory Loss," 2023). Taking care of your health is the first step toward protecting your memory. Beyond that, it's important to utilize some prevention strategies to keep your brain strong.

Prevention Strategies

Is it possible to prevent memory loss? The answer is *yes!* Preventative measures are the best way to ensure your brain stays healthy for a long time. The best preventive methods are ("Memory," n.d.b.):

- exercise

- adequate sleep

- treatment of underlying conditions

- socialization

In addition, methods of brain engagement, like mental exercises, can help improve your mental skills (Watson, 2016). These include things like puzzles, reading, playing games, and mental challenges.

Once you notice signs of cognitive decline—don't fret! It's not too late. With the right exercises and dedication, you can improve your brainpower and even reverse some damage (Timsit, 2023).

In addition to taking care of your health, it's important to seek professional help through your healthcare provider. They can prescribe medication for degenerative brain diseases or help treat underlying conditions that might be causing memory loss ("Memory Loss," 2023).

How to Use This Book

Throughout this book, there are 35 activities to improve memory and brain functioning for those struggling with, or wanting to prevent, dementia, Alzheimer's, cognitive impairments, Parkinson's, and other neurodegenerative diseases. No matter what you might be experiencing with your cognitive function now, you can find help throughout the readings to improve memory, strengthen awareness, and explore parts of your brain that have been neglected.

Does it Work?

No matter what diagnoses or other struggles have been thrust into your life, you have the ability to strengthen your brain power. Though it can be scary to struggle with memory loss, you can find success through the practical tips and methods shared in the readings.

It doesn't take extensive neurological comprehension to understand how to increase memory loss. With the use of some of the practical methods and ideas in the book, you will notice a difference in your memory retention.

The Layout

Throughout the book, there are seven chapters, each with a theme to help organize the activities:

- The first chapter will discuss basic activities that you can try to help recall past information and increase memory.

- The second chapter will include more outdoorsy and nature-related activities that will help improve health overall.

- The third chapter will cover baking, cooking, and other food-related memory activities so you can more easily make memory building a natural part of your life—since we all have to eat at some point!

- The fourth chapter will provide social and group activities to help you interact with others and improve cognitive functions.

- The fifth chapter encapsulates crafty and artistic adventures and activities for you to strengthen your brain by getting creative.

- The sixth chapter will discuss physical activities that help improve memory and add in some healthy physical movement.

- The last chapter will provide further activities to use throughout daily life.

Additional Tips

Take it at your own pace, and try activities based on what works well with your lifestyle. What works well for some might not be that great for others, and vice versa. Challenge yourself to try one activity a day for a month or stretch it over a longer period of time. This workbook works well with a companion journal or notebook so you can track your thoughts, ideas, or other relevant points as you work through the text.

The key is to stay consistent. The brain is an organ and not necessarily a muscle, but you can still work it out to help strengthen different functions. Cognitive decline is normal for any age, but it doesn't have to be to the point that it impacts daily life! Take control of your cognition and start these activities today.

Chapter 1:

Basic Activities for Memory Strengthening

Memory is useful in both practical and emotional ways. It's important to remember important information, like your bank account number or your debit card's PIN. Aside from basic life necessities, memories can help us travel to different times. Some memories are fond, like the sound of a loved one's voice. Others are more useful, like remembering past mistakes to ensure they don't happen again.

Improving memory starts by recognizing the importance of retaining information. Memories arise in all parts of the brain, and our neurological network uses a catalog system to help us recall information and make emotional connections ("Memory," n.d.a.). Exercising your memory and improving mental recall is important to do on a consistent basis to strengthen cognitive function as a whole.

In each chapter, there are trivia questions and activities to help you tap into all areas of your brain. The first chapter will provide some warm-up exercises to tap into memories and ignite your brain in its entirety. Remember to take the activities at your own pace and use an accompanying journal if necessary.

Trivia

Pick the correct answer below. The answers are at the end of the section.

Which band had the highest number of record sales in the year 1973?

A. Led Zeppelin

B. The Rolling Stones

C. Pink Floyd

D. The Beatles

What date was President John F. Kennedy assassinated as he rode in his presidential motorcade next to his wife, Jacqueline Kennedy?

A. August 1st, 1962

B. November 22, 1963

C. November 12, 1963

D. April 22, 1964

What 1992 film won Best Picture at the Oscars that year?

A. The Prince of Tides

B. Dances with Wolves

C. Unforgiven

D. The Silence of the Lambs

Which baseball team was NOT a World Series champion in the 1980s?

A. New York Mets

B. St. Louis Cardinals

C. San Francisco Giants

D. Los Angeles Dodgers

What country were the Olympics held in the year 2000?

A. Australia

B. Japan

C. Greece

D. United States

Answer Key

Which band had the highest number of record sales in the year 1973?

Answer: C. Pink Floyd topped the charts with over 50 million record sales in the year 1973 for their album *Dark Side of the Moon*.

What date was President John F. Kennedy assassinated as he rode in his presidential motorcade next to his wife, Jacqueline Kennedy?

Answer: B. November 22, 1963, was the date JFK was fatally shot in Texas.

What 1992 film won Best Picture at the Oscars that year?

Answer: D. *The Silence of the Lambs* won Best Picture in 1992, making it the first horror movie to win the award.

Which baseball team was NOT a World Series champion in the 1980s?

Answer: C. The San Francisco Giants played in the World Series in 1989 but ultimately lost to Oakland Athletics; however, they eventually became World Series champions in 2010.

What country were the Olympics held in the year 2000?

Answer: A. Australia was the country to host the Summer Olympics in the year 2000.

Activities

Staying fit doesn't require a gym membership. Mental fitness is just as important as maintaining your physical health! According to Harvard Health Publishing, "Challenging your brain with mental exercise is believed to activate processes that help maintain individual brain cells and stimulate communication among them ("6 Simple Steps," 2020)."

Are you ready to feel more mentally rejuvenated? Below are 5 activities to help kickstart your brain and boost memory retention.

My Story

Everyone has a story. What does yours look like?

As we move through life, it's easy to forget certain things we have experienced. Our past simply becomes part of our story, and while we are living in new chapters, we often forget about what happened in the beginning as the reminders of what once was fade away. This activity involves creating a mini autobiography to help you remember certain parts of your life. There are many benefits to recalling past situations. For starters, you can often relive fond memories. It's nice to recall holidays, birthdays, and other special occasions that you spent with loved ones. In addition, memories help you learn important life lessons. You can look back and reflect on past situations you've been through and find something new that you didn't realize until later on. Most importantly, going back through old memories helps you strengthen your ability to retain information. In general, this activity is focused on activating your long-term memory. While it might seem as though you don't remember certain things about your childhood, teenage, or young adult years, what you might find is as you travel through these past events, you are able to recall a lot of information.

Begin by traveling all the way back to when you were born. What was your hometown? What was your school? Do you have siblings? Who were your parents or caregivers? Did you have pets? Sometimes, reliving past memories can be painful, so don't force yourself to think about scenarios or relive situations that might be traumatic or cause you distress. You can skip over those parts for now and reevaluate them later when you feel more emotionally prepared.

For starters, focus on some of the basic information that might be included in a regular biography about yourself. What was your nickname, and what did you look like? Who were your friends? What activities did you like? Do you remember any teachers or school subjects that you did well in? Did you go on any school field trips?

Next, travel to your preteen years. What do you remember about this time in your life? Did you move houses at all? Did you go to different schools? Did you lose friends and gain new friends? Did you start participating in extracurricular activities like marching band, athletics, math club, or any other type of after-school activities?

Then, consider your high school years. Did you start dating around this time in your life, or were you not allowed to hang out with those of the opposite sex? Did you have any boyfriends or girlfriends? Did you have a big group of friends, or did you just have a small handful of people you associated with? Did you do well in school academically, or did you struggle? Did you do well athletically, or were you more focused on education? What do you remember feeling at this time? Were these fond memories that you have, or were they filled with more stressful emotions?

After, start traveling through your college years. Where did you go to school? Who did you live with? What did you study? Did you get a job right away? Did you have any pets at this time? Try to recall as much information about these different stages in your life.

Finally, you can start breaking it down in your adult years. What different careers did you have? When did you get married or start dating a partner? Did you have children? Did you go on any life-changing vacations or experience any other events that changed the direction of your life?

Once you have laid out all of your basic information, you can start to break it down year by year to help recall even more memories. Piecing your life together will create a strong mental catalog, making it easier to foster neurological connections and information recall.

What did you do when you were 10, 11, and 12 years old? What did you do when you were 21, 22, or 23 years old? What did you do in your 30s, 40s, and beyond? Traveling through your autobiography will help you remember things that you forgot even happened. You might suddenly remember a person that you haven't talked to in decades. In an instant, a memory might come flooding back to your brain that you hadn't thought about since it actually happened in your childhood. Our memories are stored in our brains like heirlooms in an attic, and now it's time to blow the dust off of them and explore them in a new light.

Again, if this is painful for you at any time, it's okay to walk away from those memories and focus on the good ones. You don't have to torture or torment yourself trying to recall every last detail. The important thing to remember about this activity is that as you start to recall information, more will come to the surface. Once you begin digging for certain bits of information, you'll find a lot of other treasures buried in your mind as well.

Image Recall

After viewing a certain image, it can be easy for the mind to forget small details quickly. Pictures blur together, and sometimes, our mind fills in the blanks. A room with red walls might transform into a room with yellow walls in your memories. You might not remember the specific color of a wall, but you do remember that the room was painted a bold color. When meeting a new person, you might not remember exactly what they look like until you see them for a second time.

To help strengthen your cognitive recall, you can increase your awareness of the presence. One way to do this is with the following image recall activity.

Below are five images. Each of them includes some detailed pictures filled with small items or textures to pay attention to. How this works is by first setting a timer for 60 seconds. During that time, spend all 60 seconds studying the image. Notice the shapes, colors, number of items, arrangement of items, and other details about each picture.

After the 60 seconds are up, you will be presented with three questions. Answer them as best as you can. The first three image questions are multiple-choice, but the last two don't have choices and are instead left for you to answer on your own as an additional challenge.

Do your best to respond based on the information you remember. Remember to set your timer for 60 seconds for each image—don't try to study all of them at once. Instead, take it one at a time and avoid reading the questions before you study the image to prevent yourself from focusing on one singular thing.

Soak in the image as best as you can. When you're ready, get started by studying the images below:

Image #1:

Image #1 Questions:

How many apples were in the picture?

    A. 2

    B. 1

    C. There were no apples

What was the fruit in?

    A. A box

    B. A bowl

    C. A coffee mug

What texture was the background?

    A. Metal

    B. Grass

    C. Wood

Answers:

    1. A

    2. B.

    3. C.

Image #2:

Image #2 Questions:

Were there clouds in the sky?

    A. Yes

    B. No

    C. The sky was covered by an umbrella

How many seagulls were in the picture?

    A. 3

    B. 4

    C. 2

What color were the stripes of the chair?

    A. Blue and white

    B. Yellow and white

    C. Blue, green, and white

Answers:

    1. A.

    2. B.

    3. A.

Image #3:

Image #3 Questions:

Which item was NOT on the table?

    A. A potted plant

    B. Gardening gloves

    C. A frog statue

What color was the water pitcher?

    A. Pink

    B. White

    C. Yellow

What color was the flower on the seed packet?

A. Blue

B. Pink

C. Green

Answers:

1. C.

2. C.

3. B.

Image #4:

Image #4 Questions:

What was the animal in the bottom right corner?

What was the color of the roof of the dollhouse?

_____

Were there stairs in the dollhouse?

_____

Answer:

1. An owl

2. Green

3. Yes

Image #5:

Image #5 Questions:

What color eyes did the kitten in the middle have?

_____

How many kittens had stripes?

_____

How many kitten's tails could you see in the image?

_____

Answers:

1. Blue

2. All five

3. None

Pictures Memory

A picture is worth a thousand words, and many of those are memories.

This activity is more focused on short-term memory. Many of us have likely played the game of Memory before. This involves placing cards facedown and flipping them one by one to find matches. However, for this book, this activity is a little different from the classic game.

Here are the steps for setting up the game:

1. Start by picking eight of your favorite pictures. These might be pictures of your family members, pets, or even pictures from the internet. You might find funny images or photos of celebrities or musicians you like. Pick eight different pictures and print them on paper. If you don't have access to a printer in your home or at your local library, you can also consider *drawing* eight different pictures.

2. Next, make a copy of each. The copies should be exact matches to make them easier to play the game with.

3. Print or cut the pictures to be the same size. Square shapes work best for this activity. These will then become your playing cards.

4. When you're finished, you should have two copies of eight different pictures, meaning that in total, you will have 16 different playing cards. Shuffle these up as best as you can.

5. Next, place the entire deck facedown. Shuffle once more.

6. Now, lay the pictures down in four-by-four tiles. This means you will lay four playing cards down and then repeat for three more rows.

Now it's time to play the actual game! These are the rules:

1. Flip one card over and study the image.

2. Flip a second card over. If they match, remove those two cards and set them aside. If they don't match, flip both cards over.

3. Draw again, following the same steps, until you've matched all of the cards.

This uses your short-term memory because you have to remember the position of each card as you flip it. This is a great activity to play with other people. You can take turns playing with grandchildren, friends, or other family members. You can also have other people provide pictures as well.

Try to challenge yourself by doing this once a day or take it to the next level by switching up the pictures or adding even more. The important thing is that they should be an even number so that you can create appropriate tiles.

You can also try creating different patterns. You might arrange them in a circle or shape like a flower. This is an extra layer that challenges your mindset even more.

The more that you consistently practice strengthening your short-term memory, the easier it will be to recall and store important and relevant information in the future.

Create a Map

One thing that makes recalling information easier is the use of a visual aid. Have you ever been in a space and suddenly memories came flooding back to you? Perhaps it was a restaurant or a friend's house. Sometimes, you don't recall information until you are in a specific area.

For this activity, you will create a map to help you bring forth more memories. This will help you strengthen your cognition and provide a physical structure to return to in the future to help you keep track of your mindset. This activity involves creating a map of a specific location from the past.

Examples of good locations to create a map of include:

- an old school

- your childhood home

- your childhood bedroom

- an old classroom

- a friend's house

- the first home that you purchased

- where you lived when you were in college

- your favorite store as a child

- a restaurant you used to visit frequently

Any type of location that used to be a relevant part of your life can be very helpful in recalling certain bits of information. To do this, start by grabbing a piece of paper. Grid paper can be especially helpful when creating your map. Start by outlining the basic structure from a bird's eye view. Pretend as though you are creating a blueprint for this location. This includes noting any different rooms, hallways, the location of doors and windows, and other large pieces of furniture.

Once you have created a basic blueprint for this activity, then create more detailed maps of smaller rooms within the vicinity. For example, if you were creating a map of your childhood home, make a blueprint of each room. To make it even more detailed, create maps of the things within each room. If you were doing something like your bedroom, create a map of the things that you might have kept on your dresser, for example. Where was the rug? Did you have toys or stuffed animals in your bedroom? Where was the closet, and what kinds of things might you have found in that closet?

You can create a map for multiple different places to help you piece together your memory. You don't have to be a perfect artist to create a memory map. Keep your collection in a binder or notebook so that you have a place to return to when you are struggling to recall information. For example, you might create a basic map of your neighborhood. Then, when you are trying to remember the name of your childhood best friend, you open up this map and visually go to their house. You can spend some time trying to recall their house, and maybe the name of your childhood friend will pop into your mind.

Having a physical visual aid can assist in recalling information. You might not be able to return to these locations, especially if they no longer exist or if they are across the country. However, you can travel there in your mindset with the use of these visual aids. In addition to this memory map, you might create a basic timeline of your life. You can use those bits of information from the "My Story" activity and create a mental roadmap that travels through all of these events.

The important thing to remember about this activity is to simply create a visual aid that can assist you when you are trying to recall information. As you are creating this map, it will also help to bring more past experiences to the surface.

Memory Prompts

In school, what is one thing teachers often had you do during lessons? Taking notes was a common activity. This is helpful for learners as it reinforces the information being taken in. You're more likely to remember what you're told if you write it down, or at least go back over it someway again later on. This would ensure that it sticks in your brain.

As an adult, journaling is a great way to help you recall, remember, and reinforce information. It's helpful to try and make journaling a regular part of your day. Set aside at least 15 minutes in the morning or at night specifically for journaling. This will ensure you can make memory journaling a regular part of your routine. Use a physical journal, like a notebook, or consider creating one on the computer. Whatever is easiest for you is best to make you more likely to journal.

Below are some journal prompts to get you started. You can answer them simply with just a few sentences. Alternatively, you can write a long journal entry for each that spans multiple pages. It's entirely up to you! The point is to get your memory jogging and help you practice reinforcement. Take them at your own pace and explore your mind!

1. What is something you have always valued?

2. What has been the most important life lesson you've learned so far?

3. What is a life lesson you wish you would have learned much sooner?

4. What is something you are the most grateful for?

5. What is a life regret you struggle with?

6. If you had a time machine and could only go back for one hour, what time would you pick?

7. What is your ideal breakfast?

8. What is a favorite food you used to enjoy as a child?

9. When was the last time you fell in love?

10. What is the best part of your day?

11. Which season was your favorite as a child, and is it the same as an adult?

12. Who was your childhood best friend?

13. When was the last time you stepped outside your comfort zone?

14. What is something you used to be afraid of but aren't anymore?

15. What has been the biggest constant in your life?

16. What is something you learned about your childhood that you could only understand as an adult?

17. What do you know about your grandparent's life?

18. What was your favorite subject in school? What was your best subject? Were these the same thing?

19. What has always been your biggest priority?

20. What was your favorite holiday as a child?

21. What is your best birthday-related memory?

22. What is the best gift you ever received from someone else?

23. How did you celebrate your 10th birthday?

24. How did you celebrate your 21st birthday?

25. Do you remember the first wedding you ever attended?

26. What do you remember about your childhood babysitter?

27. What was the most embarrassing moment of your childhood or teenage years?

28. What is the biggest challenge you overcame in your life?

29. What is one thing you thought would happen as a child that never did?

30. What is the nicest thing anyone has ever done for you?

31. What is the most scared you've ever been?

32. Who is the funniest person you know?

33. What is a moment you wish you could relive?

34. What time in your life did you have to be the strongest?

35. What is something you gave up on, and do you regret doing so?

36. What is a goal you hope to achieve in the future?

37. Who was your biggest inspiration growing up?

38. What has given your life the most meaning or purpose?

39. What scent makes you nostalgic, and what memories does it trigger?

40. Did you have a treehouse, clubhouse, or other secret spot as a child?

41. What is an item that you have had for the longest out of all your other possessions?

42. When was a time you had a big fight with your parents?

43. Do you recall the time that you laughed the most at once?

44. What do you remember most about your childhood neighbors?

45. How many vacations have you been on?

46. What is the best home-cooked meal you had, and who made it?

47. If you could have one toy you had from your childhood, what would you choose?

48. Do you remember your childhood best friend's parents? What do you remember most about them?

49. What scars do you have, and do you remember how you got them all?

50. What is your all-time favorite memory?

In Summary

Not only are puzzles and activities important for mental strength, but so is emotional management. Reducing stress and finding ways to relax will help improve your brain power ("Staying Health," 2021). Participating in these activities on a consistent basis can help you feel better overall, allowing you more mental energy to dedicate to the things you love. Keep practicing similar activities to help your brain stay active.

Chapter 2:

Outdoor Activities

Nature is all around us, but it's easy to fall out of touch with it. Between phones and TVs, there are plenty of things to keep us busy inside. However, when we don't spend enough time outdoors, we can feel disconnected from the world around us which leads to feelings of isolation and loneliness. It's good for the mind and body to get adequate fresh air and feel the natural stress-relieving effects of Mother Nature.

What's important to remember is that nature has many benefits for our health, especially when it comes to memory retention. In fact, nature has been proven to ("Going Outside," 2008):

- increase attention span

- boost memory performance

- strengthen short-term memory

Walking outside makes us happier, healthier individuals. When our health is improved as a whole, it makes it easier to stay on top of cognitive functioning. Many activities throughout the book can be taken outdoors to get an added boost of green therapy.

Trivia

Pick the correct answer below. The answers are at the end of the section.

What is the most common tree in North America?

A. Hackberry

B. Sycamore

C. Douglas Fir

D. Red Maple

Which animal below is NOT an omnivore?

A. Racoon

B. Cat

C. Fox

D. Skunk

What is the coldest planet in our solar system?

A. Saturn

B. Neptune

C. Mars

D. Pluto

How many types of insect species are there estimated to be in the world?

A. 900,000

B. 9,000,000,000

C. 9,000,000

D. 90,000

Which is not a type of algae?

A. Marimo

B. Seaweed

C. Lily-pads

D. Kelp

Answer Key

What is the most common tree in North America?

Answer: D. The Red Maple is often considered the most common tree in North America.

Which animal below is NOT an omnivore?

Answer: B. Cats are considered carnivorous and mostly feed on prey, whereas the others are omnivorous and sometimes opportunistic feeders, meaning they feed on both plants and animals.

What is the coldest planet in our solar system??

Answer: B. Neptune is the oldest planet, with temperatures reaching as low as -300 degrees Fahrenheit.

How many types of insect species are there estimated to be in the world?

Answer: A. 900,000 insect species are estimated to exist according to The Smithsonian, with insects accounting for 80 percent of species in existence ("Numbers of Insects," n.d)).

Which is not a type of algae?

Answer: C. Lily-pads are not considered algae and are a type of aquatic plant.

Activities

Whenever you step outside of your home or office and into a green space, you are opening up your mind to the natural world. Spending time in nature has been shown to provide relaxing effects and increase concentration, creativity, and problem-solving skills ("3 Ways," 2023).

The activities below will help you connect to your natural roots and feel the benefits of the great outdoors.

Create a Birdhouse

Nature is beautiful, but it's easy to ignore that beauty and instead spend more time inside, especially in modern times. When we're indoors, we often have many things that we can use as distractions, like televisions, books, and other forms of entertainment. However, there's plenty of entertainment outside so we just have to know how to find it. One great way to do this is through the use of a birdhouse. A birdhouse or a bird feeder is a great activity to help you get crafty while also ensuring that you spend more time outdoors.

This activity involves first purchasing or building a birdhouse. Many craft stores have wooden birdhouses ready for you to paint and decorate as you please. If you would rather create one from scratch, you can use many different types of materials at home. For example, you can use an old milk carton or plastic bottle. Simply cut a hole in the side and tie a string around the top. You can then fill the birdfeeder with types of seeds or other treats for the birds.

Once you've decided what type of birdhouse to use, hang it from your favorite tree and sit outside and watch as they flock to the food. This can provide an endless amount of entertainment.

If you choose to decorate your own, get creative with the way that it looks. For example, create a bird restaurant or a bird camper. Whichever way you choose to decorate your bird feeder is up to you.

When picking a spot, ensure it is in a spot where you can easily sit from a distance and watch the birds. Hang it from a tree or outside one of your windows. One important tip to remember is to be conscious of anything that might fall from the bird feeder. For example, seeds can sometimes fall, and they might actually grow into a plant if they land in the soil beneath the feeder. In addition, excessive amounts of fallen food could attract ground rodents such as mice.

However, this shouldn't deter you from still using a birdhouse, as it's a great way to give back to nature while providing you with entertainment. Sit outside patiently as you wait for the birds to start arriving. You might also find that you have some squirrel friends who want to check out the different treats you provide to the birds.

Write down any types of birds that you see and take pictures so that you can do more research on what types of birds have been visiting your area. Notice the feeding rituals they have and how long they spend there, and pay attention to any types of treats that they seem to enjoy more than others. As your excitement grows around these visiting friends, you will find yourself spending more time outdoors.

This activity also helps to keep you mindful in the moment. When birdwatching, you pay attention to the birds as they travel to and from the birdhouse, and you also create memories. This can strengthen your cognitive abilities while also ensuring you are spending plenty of time outdoors.

From Seed to Plant

There is much to learn from nature. Watching life grow from a seed into a fruiting plant is an inspiring fascination. This next activity involves utilizing this natural growth to your memory benefit.

Watching the transformation will help you check in daily and stay mindful of time as it passes. You will have a physical point that you can use to reflect back to in the future. Tracking progress is exciting and adds a little brightness to your day.

To start, you will need:

- a sunny spot

- 3 or more pots varying in size

- a drip tray

- soil

- a seed

- a water source

- (optional) fertilizer

Ensure you pick a seed that is easy to grow for beginners. These include plants like tomatoes, sunflowers, or beans.

Plant your seed in a small pot first, and increase the pot size as it grows. The instructions are as follows:

1. Fill your pot with soil without packing it down too much.

2. Dig a small hole the size of the seed around half an inch deep.

3. Place the seed in the hole and cover with soil.

4. Water lightly, just enough to soak the soil without it overflowing.

5. Water daily until you have an established plant, then water accordingly based on the seed packet's instructions.

It's a good idea to plant a few seeds at once, as not all seeds will make it, despite your strongest green thumb.

Once the plant has established a few leaves and is five or more inches tall, you can transfer it to a larger pot. Continue to increase the pot size as the plant grows, or plant it directly in the ground if you have an outdoor space.

Because plants require frequent check-ins, this is a great activity to keep your memory sharp. You can set daily timers to remind you to check in and ensure it doesn't need watered or a new, sunnier spot.

Choosing an edible plant will also help improve your culinary skills. There's nothing quite like a homecooked meal with homegrown ingredients or a fresh bouquet picked from your very own garden!

Count the Stars

Cloud-gazing is a popular activity that is a fun pastime to help enjoy the bright blue sky. But just as beautiful is the sky after the sun has set. There are many memory-boosting benefits to an activity like stargazing because it is an outdoor activity that requires mindfulness. When you step outside and crane your neck to see the twinkling ceiling of the earth, you are presented with an endless sea of thought, much of which can work out different areas of your brain.

Stargazing can also be beneficial if you struggle with falling asleep at night. Our bodies follow a natural rhythm, The Circadian rhythm, based on the level of light we are exposed to throughout the day. This is why the sunrise wakes us up, and a dark sky can make us more tired. However, artificial light can trick our subconscious into thinking it's a different time of day. This means if you're up all night staring at a big TV screen, you might find yourself struggling to get sleepy well into the night. Exposing yourself to the night sky will remind your mind that it's time to transition into sleep mode.

To stargaze, find a place outdoors that you feel safe in, with access to the night sky. The only rule is to gaze at the stars! At first, you might find your mind races with other thoughts. To help distract yourself, try counting the stars. Count to 10 first, then to 25, 50, and 100. Eventually, you will find that your mind starts to slow down, helping you to reduce stress in the process.

Additional tips:

- If you have the means to do so, consider purchasing a telescope as a way to enhance your stargazing sessions.

- Do you see any planes traveling? Consider where they might be headed or leaving from.

- Stargaze while you are chatting to a friend in person or on the phone.

- Make a cup of warm tea to help increase the stress-relieving benefits of stargazing.

- Use this time outdoors as one to journal or wind down with a mind puzzle like sudoku or trivia.

Some common constellations and other things to look for include:

- **The big dipper:** This is a common constellation that resembles a cup or bowl with a handle. You can spot this by identifying four stars that make a trapezoid, followed by three additional stars that make the handle.

- **The moon:** The moon isn't visible every night, but depending on the phase and location, you can see the moon with the naked eye. Track the different phases and see if you can spot the moon each night.

- **Other planets:** While they can be confused with other stars, many planets are visible, like Jupiter or Saturn. According to the Adler Planetarium, " stars twinkle and planets don't ("How to Identify," 2020)."

When we look at the simplest aspects of the world around us, we can realize just how complex they really are.

Paint a Scene

Nature has been one of the greatest inspirations for art throughout history. From picturesque paintings to abstract displays, the natural occurrence of plants, animals, water, mountains, and other relevant landscape aspects are inspiring and beautiful. This activity involves selecting one of your favorite scenes and taking the time to paint it.

The supplies that you will need are your canvas or a piece of paper, paints, and paintbrushes. You might also want to invest in an easel or choose a location that has a table for you to sit at so that you have something to hold your medium as you are crafting this landscape painting.

Utilize a bag or briefcase to help you carry your supplies. Ensure that you select an area that you feel safe and comfortable in for a long period of time. For example, hiking to the middle of the woods without access to a bathroom or water source might be challenging. Paintings can take a long time, so it's important that you choose a location where you can sit for an extended artistic session.

Once you have found the perfect and most picturesque location, it is time to start painting. Begin by painting your canvas a blank white. If you're using watercolors, you can skip this step. Painting a canvas with your selected medium is a great way to get the canvas wet so it's easier to work with.

Next, you will want to create the shadows of the basic scene. This means creating a basic black or brown silhouette of the main structures that you're going to be working with. This will make it easier for you to plan out your painting and know where everything is going to be placed. This means painting any trees or other big structures that are going to be in your painting.

Following this, start to fill out the correct colors of the basic trees and other buildings or structures within the landscape painting. This means selecting the right blues for your sky or water or picking the right greens for grass and pastures.

After that, you will want to focus on creating the more detailed aspect of your painting. Add reflections, small shadows, and other things that really bring the painting to life. Painting is all about crafting something in layers, and that starts with the background. The basic structures, the correct colors, and the details of the painting are the layers on top. As you create your different layers, pay attention to how things are connected, as well as the different shapes and intricacies of everything that you paint. By the time you are finished, you will have a beautiful scene that will help you memorialize this time in your life.

Tree Hunting

There are trees all around us, and if we fail to pay attention, we miss some of their beauty. This activity sets out to help you reacquaint yourself with nature, helping to grow your brain power in the process.

First, identify some common types of trees in your area. Look up what types of maple, fir, or elm trees might be frequently found in your area. This will vary from region to region, so it's up to you to look into what species are native to your geographical location.

Once you have an idea of what trees to look for, the next important step is to get out in nature and start looking! To identify trees, there are a few tips to follow:

- **Start with the leaves.** Are they big and round, or thin, with many different shapes? The leaves are the first sign to look for.

- **Don't overlook their bark.** The textures in the bark and color can be very telling of what type of tree you might be looking at.

- **Consider their size.** Some trees only grow a certain height, whereas others are known for being large and expansive.

Try to find at least three different types of trees in your area. Then, check in with them once a season. How do they change and transform? Which loses their leaves first, and which has the prettiest color? Do any of them have flowers in the spring? Do they grow fruit in the summer? As you grow your knowledge of these trees, you will start to learn much more about other types of trees.

Going on nature walks and connecting to the world around you can reduce stress and increase your attention span, making it easier to grow a strong memory.

In Summary

Nature is beautiful. It is an inspiration and can force us to think more creatively. The more time you are able to spend outside, the more you expose your mind to the benefits of nature. Even when you are not focused on brain-boosting activities, do your best to get outdoors. Eat meals, read books, and simply sit outside in the great outdoors. You will find that your health improves overall, making it easier to concentrate on the things that matter the most.

Chapter 3:

Improving Memory in the Kitchen

What you choose to eat can greatly impact how your brain functions. Food is fuel, so knowing the right things to eat will ensure your brain is properly energized. This chapter has food-related activities so you can make the most of your memory-improvement journey and allow these skills to expand in the culinary sense.

Whenever choosing foods or meals, focus on brain-boosting foods to help strengthen your cognition. Foods that are good for your brain include (Jennings, 2023):

- broccoli

- oranges

- seeds and nuts

- berries

- eggs

- green tea and coffee

Not only are the actual vitamins and nutrients in foods memory-boosting, but the senses they trigger can also strengthen our brains. For example, smelling something like apple pie might take you back to mom's kitchen, or maybe the smell of a certain candle reminds you of a different time. When you're able to focus on memory improvement in different areas of everyday life, you give your brain the opportunity to make mental exercise a more natural part of your routine.

Trivia

Pick the correct answer below. The answers are at the end of the section.

Which below is a type of soft cheese?

    A. Brie

    B. Swiss

    C. Parmesan

    D. Asiago

What is the most popular ice cream flavor in the United States?

    A. Strawberry

    B. Chocolate

    C. Vanilla

    D. Peanut Butter

How many burgers does the average American eat in a year?

    A. 156

    B. 52

    C. 20

    D. 114

Which of these below is not a type of apple?

    A. Golden Delicious

    B. Fuji

    C. Russet

D. Ambrosia

Which type of plant is poisonous to humans?

A. Tarragon

B. Borage

C. Calendula

D. Oleander

Answer Key

Which below is a type of soft cheese?

Answer: A. Brie has a creamy texture, making it a type of soft cheese.

What is the most popular ice cream flavor in the United States?

Answer: C. Vanilla is a classic flavor that reigns as the most popular ice cream in the U.S.

How many burgers does the average American eat in a year?

Answer: A. According to PBS, the average American eats three hamburgers weekly, totaling over 150 yearly (Cobo, 2012).

Which of these below is not a type of apple?

Answer: C. Russet is not a type of apple and instead refers to a type of potato.

Which type of herb is poisonous to humans?

Answer: D. Oleander is poisonous to humans and can even be fatal in some cases.

Activities

Try these activities for your next meal or snack. Spin the rules to suit your preferences. For example, if you like cookies over cupcakes, swap those out in the next activity. If you like vegetables more than fruit, pick those instead for the second activity. Customizing these activities will make them more relevant and, therefore, more impactful to your memory improvement.

Cupcake Decoration

Who doesn't love a little bit of cake? Whether you like chocolate, vanilla, strawberry, or carrot, cake can bring a smile to many different faces. For this activity, you are encouraged to get your cake-decorating skills fine-tuned to help strengthen your cognitive abilities.

First, select your type of cake. A boxed mix is usually the easiest, but if you have experience baking in the kitchen, then feel free to create your own culinary masterpiece from scratch. Next, utilize a cupcake tin to help you create cupcakes. You can make a whole cake if you'd like. However, cupcakes can be much easier to decorate as you have more room to practice and make mistakes. Once your cake has been baked, next, remove the cupcakes from the tins.

In three or more bowls, mix together frosting with your preferred color choice. Choose at least two colors in addition to the simple white or yellow frosting that you're using. Again, feel free to make frosting from scratch. However, if you do not have these types of culinary skills, it's perfectly fine to use store-made frosting.

Once you have your cupcakes ready to be decorated and the frosting well mixed, it is then time to get creative. Start by smearing frosting across the entire cupcake. Then, using smaller utensils or even piping bags, create more intricate designs on the cupcake. Challenge yourself with this. Create things like a smiley face, a flower, or a heart.

Think of a theme that you can also utilize to help you decorate your cupcakes. Is anyone's birthday coming? Is it the start of the season, like spring or fall? Can you decorate for holidays, such as Christmas or Valentine's Day? You can also try and spell letters on your cupcakes. You might spell Happy Birthday or Happy Easter. Consider different special occasions that you can use your cupcakes for.

Once you have finished crafting your perfect cupcakes, it's time to enjoy them. You can share them with loved ones or simply eat them yourself as a nice sweet treat. This activity helps you stay mindful in the moment because you are forced to focus on what you are doing in front of you. Any type of creative activity can also help with cognitive functioning. It forces your brain to think creatively and logically about how to execute a specific design or pattern.

Most importantly, having a sweet treat like a cupcake can make you happier. Mood-boosting activities are always good for your brain. If you don't like cupcakes, you might consider decorating something like cookies or even a pie.

Five Senses Fruit Salad

Our senses are very impactful on our cognitive functioning. The ability to see, smell, taste, touch, and hear is something that many humans are born with. As time passes, sometimes we lose some of these abilities. For example, our sight might not be what it used to be, or perhaps it's harder for us to hear things than it once was. However, that doesn't mean that we can't still strengthen and help those senses flourish.

One activity to do this is the five senses fruit salad. This is also a great activity to get you in the kitchen and help work on your health. Fruit is packed with nutrients and important vitamins, as well as hydration that is necessary for your basic bodily functions.

To start this activity, head to your local grocery store and select at least three different fruits. You can use canned fruit if you would like. However, selecting a fresh fruit will help make this activity a little bit more complex.

Next, take your fruits home and begin the process of washing and preparing them. Peel any skin that you don't want. For example, orange peels need to be removed before creating the salad. You can also drain and rinse any canned fruit that you plan to use.

Now, it is time to really explore your senses. Grab each piece of fruit and think about how it tastes, how it smells, and how it looks. How does it feel under your hand? What sound does it make as you peel or chop this fruit? Cut it into small, bite-sized pieces and toss it into a bowl.

Remember to identify your five senses with each different fruit that you add to the fruit salad. Try to add at least three, but adding more fruits into the salad gives you more opportunities to explore your five senses.

Then, once the salad is all mixed together, go through your five senses again. What does it sound like as you mix it? What does it taste like and smell like? What do you see when you look at this bowl of colorful fruit? What does it feel like as you take your first bite? Now you have a prepared fruit salad that you can enjoy for the next few days. Each time you eat this, guide yourself to be mindful and try to remember the time that it took preparing this, as well as your time at the grocery store as you're picking out these different types of fruits.

How do the tastes and shape of the fruit change over time? For example, bananas might become more mushy, or apples might become softer. Oranges might become juicier over time. Pay attention to the way that these senses transform as the fruit mixes together.

If you don't like fruit that much, you can also use vegetables to create a healthy salad. Once you chop and prepare your vegetables, toss them with pasta or lettuce and your favorite dressing for a delicious meal. The point of this activity is to help you explore your senses while also staying mindful in the kitchen. This trains your brain so that you are automatically more mindful the next time you're preparing food. You might start thinking about the way that it tastes and smells, therefore pulling your focus to what you are doing and boosting your mental abilities in the process.

Blind Taste Test

Taste is a powerful sense. The flavor of something can transform you to a different time. It can help recall memories and strengthen your mental abilities by helping to trigger prior experiences.

For this activity, you will participate in a blind taste test to help you strengthen your ability to identify intricate details within flavors. This is a great activity to try with other people, but you can also do it on your own.

To start, select one of your favorite beverages. This might be soda, juice, or maybe you even pick water. Now, select three different types of this drink. You can select different brands, or maybe you select different containers that it comes in. For example, if you select water, first select your favorite kind of water. Next, you might use tap water and third, perhaps you use a different brand of water you've never tried. If you really like lemon-lime soda, you might use three different brands of lemon-lime soda. You might use a name brand, a store brand, or a brand that you've never heard of. Alternatively, select three different containers for this drink. For example, if you really like cola, perhaps you stick to the same brand. Instead, you pick cola in a can, cola in a bottle, and cola from a fountain soda machine that you can get from your local gas station or convenience store.

Once you have your chosen beverages, select three glasses that are all the same. You can use plastic cups or glasses that you already have at home. Then, place a sticker on the bottom of each. Write down what sticker you used for what drink you'll be tasting. For example, if you use a purple, blue, and yellow sticker, place one each on the bottom of the cups or glasses, then, on a piece of paper, write down which flavor goes with which sticker. When filling your cup, make sure they are all filled the same amount so you can't differentiate which is which. Hide the piece of paper before starting, and mix up the cups so you don't know which is which.

When you're ready, blindfold yourself or simply close your eyes. Take a sip from each. Do your best to identify which flavor corresponds with which beverage. It can be very difficult when you don't know what exactly you are drinking. You might think you know exactly what one tastes like, but once you have your eyes closed and are really focusing on the flavors, it might be harder for you to differentiate between the three different types of beverages.

After you finish them and make your guesses, check your answers to see if you are correct. You will be surprised at how hard it can be to identify certain flavors.

Try this with different drinks to see how well you are able to really pay attention to the flavors within each. This activity is even more challenging when you don't even know what beverage is chosen and another partner does this process for you. Try it with chips, flavors of candy, and any other food you can think of! It's a great way to grow your brainpower by challenging your mindset to pick up on different cues within food.

Fill in the Blank

Increasing awareness in the kitchen will make mindfulness a more natural part of your life. Everyone needs to eat, so we are in the kitchen multiple times a day preparing meals or searching for snacks. One way to help you become more present in the kitchen is to define your preferences.

For this activity, you will fill in the blanks of the sentences and prompts below. These are there to help you make more sense of the things you like. By doing this, you strengthen your recall and identify your preferences. You will also be prompted to think about food on a deeper level, strengthening your relationship with the culinary arts.

Try filling in these prompts with other people, like your spouse or partner. You might end up learning new things about each other! Get as descriptive as possible. For example, instead of saying, "I like apples," use words, or multiple words, like:

- I adore apples.

- I loathe apples.

- I love the flavor and smell of apples.

- I like eating spiced apples.

- I am excited when I get to eat apples.

For the example, "My favorite cheese is..." you might fill the prompt out by saying:

- My favorite cheese is parmesan.

- My favorite cheese is gouda for cheese and crackers and pepper jack for sandwiches.

- My favorite cheese is any kind! I love cheese!

- My favorite cheese is melted mozzarella on top of pizza.

- My favorite cheese is deep-fried with a side of marinara sauce.

As you can see, you can use additional sentences and more descriptive words to get your food-related cognitive skills churning.

Fill in the blanks in the spaces provided, or rewrite the sentence in your own words in your journal:

1. I _____ apples.

2. My favorite cheese is _____.

3. I _____ pizza.

4. I like the taste of _____, but not so much the texture.

5. Encourage readers to use descriptive words, like I loathe apples, or I adore pizza.

6. The best thing on a sandwich is _____.

7. If I could only eat one flavor of chips for the rest of my life, I would choose _____.

8. If I could only have one type of _____ for the rest of my life, I would choose _____.

9. The worst meal I've ever had was _____.

10. My secret ingredient for _____ is _____.

11. I love when my best friend, _____, makes _____.

12. The best thing my parent ever made me was _____.

13. A food that instantly triggers my memory is _____.

14. The best snack to have at a party is _____.

15. _____ tastes better when you add _____.

16. _____ is my favorite food to eat with other people.

17. One food I like that other people don't often like is _____.

18. The thing I'm best at preparing is _____.

19. The one food I always seem to mess up the recipe for is _____.

20. My favorite food to order for takeout is _____, and the place that makes it the best is _____.

21. A food that I've probably eaten the most in my life is _____.

22. I put _____ on top of most of my foods.

23. The weirdest food I've ever eaten is _____.

24. The ultimate ice cream topping is _____.

25. My favorite candy is _____, and my favorite flavor is _____.

26. If I could only have one drink for the rest of my life, I would choose _____.

27. A food that smells better than it tastes is _____.

28. A food that tastes better than it smells is _____.

29. The ultimate dessert is _____.

30. If I had to give up one food that I like, I would choose _____.

31. A food I will NEVER eat is _____.

32. My LEAST favorite candy is _____.

33. I _____ dipping my fries in ketchup.

34. I always use _____ milk in my cereal.

35. The best food to eat around the holidays is _____.

Pizza Face

This activity will encourage you to create your own pizza or French bread pizza and make a face from the toppings.

First, select either store-bought dough or homemade pizza dough. You can also use French bread if you don't want to have to worry about baking any type of dough. Simply slice the French bread loaf in half and use that in place of dough.

Next, select three to five different toppings that you enjoy. Cheese and sauce are not included and should be included in addition to your chosen toppings. This means picking something like pepperoni, sausage, green pepper, red onion, spinach, bacon, mushrooms, and other types of your favorite pizza toppings.

Once you have made your selection, it's time to get baking. Now, place your dough or French bread on a pan. Cover it with sauce and then cheese. You should have a classic-looking pizza.

Now, it is time to create different faces using vegetables or meat. It's always fun when you are able to play with your food! Try creating a silly face or maybe even the face of someone you know. The point of this activity is to help you think logically and creatively while also using your culinary skills.

It can also be helpful to use memory-boosting foods like spinach or red onions that help reduce inflammation and strengthen your cognitive abilities. Bake the pizza according to the directions of the pizza dough that you used. Then, enjoy your delicious creation!

As our memories start to fade, one ability we lose is that of face recognition. Faces help us identify the people that we love, and they are often associated with many of our memories. Strengthening your ability to pay attention to a facial structure's intricacies will help boost your memory.

In Summary

Food is powerful. It shapes our health and can transform the way our body operates. Food is something you deal with every day, so make the most out of each meal and snack by relating it to your cognitive abilities.

Chapter 4:

Getting Social with Cognitive Improvement

What goes on in our minds is often something that happens internally. However, the experiences we have are also very powerful in improving cognitive function. Other people challenge us, share interesting stories and ideas, and make us think in ways we might not have on our own. This is why socializing is so important to help improve your health.

Socializing has many benefits, but in relation to memory improvement, it has been shown to ("Why is Socialization," n.d.):

- reduce stress

- increase happiness

- increase longevity

- lower dementia risk

Whether you have a big network of friends and family or you only have a handful of acquaintances, it's important to incorporate methods into your life to boost socialization. Try connecting to others with similar interests through adult classes, groups like book clubs, or even reaching out to those with similar interests online. What matters most is that you challenge your brain to think in new ways and focus on surrounding yourself with people who make you feel good.

Trivia

Pick the correct answer below. The answers are at the end of the section.

What is the estimated global population?

   A. 10 million

   B. 8 billion

   C. 900 million

   D. 30 billion

What activity do most Americans spend their free time on?

   A. Reading

   B. Socializing

   C. Watching TV

   D. Exercise

What is the most spoken language in the world?

   A. Spanish

   B. Mandarin Chinese

   C. French

   D. English

Which religion is the most practiced in the world?

   A. Judaism

   B. Buddhism

   C. Muslim

   D. Christianity

Out of the answers below, which sport is the most recently invented?

A. Tennis

B. Pickleball

C. Football

D. Paddleball

Answer Key

What is the estimated global population?

Answer: B. 8 billion is the estimated number of living people globally.

What activity do most Americans spend their free time on?

Answer: C. Watching TV is the most common pastime for both men and women in the United States ("TED," 2022).

What is the most spoken language in the world?

Answer: D. English is the most spoken language in the world.

Which religion is the most practiced in the world?

Answer: D. Christianity is the most practiced religion in the world.

Out of the answers below, which sport is the most recently invented?

Answer: D. Paddleball was invented by just a few men in 1965 after creating a game the whole family could play ("History of the Game," n.d.).

Activities

Below are some activities to try with friends, family, and others who want to improve their memory. These are great exercises to do with grandkids or your spouse or partner. Playing games with others can make you happier and reduce stress, therefore improving your cognitive abilities.

Send a Card

It always feels good to receive a card from a loved one. For this activity, you will be sending a card to someone that you know. This will help you reconnect with that person while boosting your memory in the process. You can use a card that you purchase, but for this activity, it's encouraged for you to make a card on your own.

To do this, select old scrap paper or construction paper you already have available. You can also head to your local craft store to purchase supplies if you have the means to do so. Take your piece of paper and fold it in half. Now, decorate the outside according to whatever theme you are going for. You might be sending a birthday card, holiday card, or simply a card to let someone know that you are thinking of them. You can use paints, stickers, or other things to help create a beautiful greeting card.

The second part of this activity is to write a note within the card. This is a message to help you connect to a friend or loved one. Ask how someone is doing or if anything exciting has happened in their life recently. Start by addressing the card to this person, and then write about how you are feeling or what you're thinking about.

Share what different things you have been up to and ask them questions to encourage them to write you a letter back.

Once you are done, place the card into an envelope and mail it to them. There are a few different reasons that this can help with your memory-boosting abilities. First, you are being creative when crafting the letter. Whenever you are creative, you get your brain juices flowing, making it easier for you to increase your cognitive abilities. On top of that, you are also recalling certain bits of information. Memories are easier to explore when we are sharing them with another person. If you recall certain memories that you've had with friends and family members, they might help to add details in areas where you are missing certain bits of information. This is a great way to help strengthen your relationship as well as your memory-boosting capabilities. Hopefully, the other person will mail you a letter back, and then you can start to share cards back and forth. In our digital age, it's easy to reduce physical communication with other people because we are so reliant on our cell phones, so utilizing a card is a great way to help you connect to your past in a plethora of ways.

I'm Going Camping

This activity involves at least one other person, but as many people can play as you'd like. It is a fun game to help you increase your short-term memory skills. It is called "I'm going camping."

How it works is each person takes turns stating items that they are taking camping with them. The challenge is that you have to also name all of the other things that the person before you shared.

For example, one person, Person A, starts by saying:

- I'm going camping, and I'm bringing a pillow.

The next person, Person B, then repeats this and adds their own item. They would then say:

- I'm going camping, and I'm bringing a pillow and a blanket.

After this, a third person, Person C (or the first person if playing with two people), adds a third item. They would then say:

- I'm going camping, and I'm bringing a pillow, a blanket, and a lantern.

Then, it goes back to the next person. A typical game might continue like this:

- Person A: I'm going camping, and I'm bringing a pillow, a blanket, a lantern, and firewood.

- Person B: I'm going camping, and I'm bringing a pillow, a blanket, a lantern, firewood, and marshmallows.

- Person C: I'm going camping, and I'm bringing a pillow, a blanket, a lantern, firewood, marshmallows, and a camping chair.

- Person A: I'm going camping, and I'm bringing a pillow, a blanket, a lantern, firewood, marshmallows, a camping chair, and a book.

- Person B: I'm going camping, and I'm bringing a pillow, a blanket, a lantern, firewood, marshmallows, a camping chair, a book, and hiking shoes.

- Person C: I'm going camping, and I'm bringing a pillow, a blanket, a lantern, firewood, marshmallows, a camping chair, a book, hiking shoes, and a hat.

This repeats back and forth until somebody forgets an item or gets it wrong.

This forces you to use your short-term memory because you have to sit there and store all of those items so that you can easily recall them once again.

Repeat this activity in several different ways. You don't always have to say that you're going camping. For example, you might say, "I'm going to the beach." This would then look like:

- I'm going to the beach, and I'm bringing a towel.

- I'm going to the beach, and I'm bringing a towel and a swimsuit.

- I'm going to the beach, and I'm bringing a towel, a swimsuit, and sunscreen.

Repeat this activity and see how many times you and the other person can go before one of you forgets. This is a great game to play with grandkids! If you find that you mess up or you feel embarrassed in front of your grandkids, make it a silly and forgetful moment to prompt the child to help you remember.

Other types of prompts might be:

- I'm going grocery shopping, and I need to buy...

- I'm going to the theater, and I'm going to watch a movie that has...

- I'm going hunting or fishing and taking...

- I'm going shopping and the mall and want to purchase...

- I'm going on vacation and will take...

- I'm going on a hike...

- I'm going to go get ice cream, and on top of my ice cream, I'm going to add...

- I'm going to make a pizza, and on top of my pizza, I'm going to add...

There are many opportunities to get creative with this activity, so try changing it up each time you play. The answers don't always have to be logical. It's better to just say what comes to mind rather than trying to be accurate. For example, you might say, I'm going grocery shopping and need to buy... an elephant! Sometimes, the funnier the answer, the easier it is to remember.

Birthday Book

Birthdays are a great time of the year to celebrate with other people and reconnect with those you cherish the most. Socializing consistently throughout the year is important, so birthdays and other special occasions are a great reason to connect with somebody else.

You can reach out through social media or celebrate the birthday by taking the birthday girl or boy out to dinner.

This activity involves creating a scrapbook with a page or two dedicated to each month. Each month will then cover different people whose birthday falls within that month. You can then decorate each page using the full person's name and date of birth. You might even include the time while they were born and other small details about this person. You can list some of the things that they like or dislike. This is especially helpful so that you know what you might be able to get them for their birthday in the future!

For example, for a month like March, your nephew John and neighbor Sarah's birthdays fall on days within that month. You can list that John likes tractors and fishing, and Sarah likes flowers and baked goods. You then know when it's their birthday month and what day it falls so you can wish them a happy birthday or send them a card. You also have a few ideas for potential gifts to give them if you have the means to do so.

Each month in the birthday book will have everybody listed within that month, so you always know whose birthday is coming up.

You can also include other special occasions if you'd like. For example, you might include your children's wedding anniversaries or your grandchildren's graduation dates. This is a great way to help keep your memory strong and have a point of reference to go to in the future.

Movie Club

You've likely heard of a book club before, but a movie club is an alternative way to help connect with others while also exploring things that boost your cognitive abilities. Movies are very visual things. They are filled with dialog, stories, characters, and other interesting elements that all take attention and focus to be able to comprehend.

When you are able to sit through a movie, you are able to unlock different parts of your brain. You have to use creative and logical thinking when trying to figure out mysteries and other aspects of a thriller. You feel good and are happy during a comedy film and other funny scenes in a movie. You might also be transported to a different time while watching an old movie or a period piece.

Creating a movie club is a great way to connect with others while also forcing yourself to dive into the cinematic universe in a brand-new way. This activity involves starting a movie club. You are encouraged to gather a few friends or family members and dedicate one night a week or a month (depending on your schedule) to watch a movie. After you watch the movie, you will then discuss it with the other person.

You can also add in other activities to help make this experience even more exciting. For example, you might choose a movie that was filmed in your city. Then you can go on a tour of the different locations where this movie was filmed. You might have everyone bring snacks that are related to the movie. You could even have everyone dressed up as a character in that movie.

You can also set different rules for the movie club. For example, you might have everyone take turns picking a movie each week. You might have everyone suggest a couple of movies, and then everybody votes on the movie to decide what you will be watching. The only rule for this is that you can't vote for your own movie.

There can also be themes. For example, one week, you might have a thriller theme. The next week, it might be a romance theme. You can even pick a movie that was made after a book, combining it with a book club.

Movies can be easier commitments for people to participate in than books. When in a book club, you have to read the book outside of the time that you are gathering with the club, which could require much more time than a movie.

When you have a movie club, it only takes a few hours out of your week, or even month, to get together and watch that movie and then have a discussion afterward. This can make everybody more likely or even more willing to participate. You can even do the movie club with younger individuals and choose family-friendly movies. Discuss the different elements of the movie. What was the most exciting part? What do you think was a bad decision in that movie? Was there a scene that should have been deleted? Was the movie confusing? Did you understand it well? Were there deeper themes or meanings behind the movie that you might not have initially picked up on? This is a great way to help you connect socially while also increasing your learning abilities.

Instructions Challenge

The instructions challenge activity is a fun way for you to connect with another person. Start by finding a small task you can do with another person. To do the activity, one person is blindfolded while they perform the task, and the other person should give them instructions to complete that task. It's a fun and silly challenge to get you to think about how you give and take instructions.

This challenges your brain, therefore strengthening your logical thinking skills. For example, one simple task might be to make a peanut butter and jelly sandwich. Person A would then be blindfolded and stand in front of the table (using safe utensils, of course). It's suggested to use spoons or spatulas rather than a knife for activities like this.

Person A is blindfolded and stands there ready, awaiting instructions. Person B has a full view of the scene, but they cannot actually use their hands in this activity. They're simply observers who are giving instructions. Person A is then supposed to follow the instructions as closely as possible. This means if Person B says, "Put the peanut butter on the bread," Person A might literally take the jar of peanut butter and set it on top of the loaf of bread while both are still packaged.

There are so many small details that are required in the instructions. This activity would involve instructions like:

- Open the bag of bread.

- Pull out a piece of bread.

- Place it on a plate.

- Grab your spatula.

- Open the container of peanut butter.

- Scoop out some peanut butter with your spatula.

- Spread that peanut butter on the bread.

As you can see, this is a much more intricate and detailed step-by-step guide rather than simply saying, "Put the peanut butter on the bread."

Other tasks to consider are:

- Put on a sock.

- Write your name on a piece of paper.

- Tie a shoe.

- Pour a bowl of cereal.

- Wash a dish.

The point of this challenge is to get as detailed as possible with your instructions. You might find that the other person ends up doing something silly or taking your instructions in the wrong way, which can make the activity even more exciting. It's a great thing to do with spouses or children to help strengthen your bond and use up some of your free time.

In Summary

Loneliness has been associated with cognitive decline ("Mayo Clinic," 2019). Some of us can't socialize as we might not have the ability to get out of the house often, but even connecting to others online can help. In addition, consider adopting a pet, as they can help provide a companion who you can talk and spend time with. We are all humans with similar needs, one of those being social connection ("Why Socialization is Essential," n.d.). Do what you can to help strengthen bonds and friendships for your memory.

Chapter 5:

Exploring the Creative Part of Your Brain

Creativity is an important part of cognitive function. When we are forced to look at things from a new perspective, challenging our mindset in the process. Thinking creatively strengthens the bonds and connections in your brain ("The Power," n.d.). This means that you enhance the network of your brain overall when you participate in creative activities. Once those connections are strengthened, it then becomes easier to utilize your memory.

Everyone has the ability to be creative. Sometimes it just requires a little extra challenge on our part. The activities in this chapter will help you explore your artistic side so you can activate different creative regions of your brain.

Trivia

Pick the correct answer below. The answers are at the end of the section.

Which of the following is NOT a type of paint?

    A. Oil

    B. Acetone

    C. Watercolor

    D. Acrylic

Which artist was born in 1853?

    A. Jackson Pollock

    B. Rembrandt

C. Vincent van Gogh

D. Pablo Picasso

Who painted the ceiling of the Sistine Chapel?

A. Leonardo da Vinci

B. Michelangelo

C. Donatello

D. Giotto

Which of the following is NOT a shade of green?

A. Emerald

B. Forest

C. Chartreuse

D. Magenta

Where is the largest art museum in the world located?

A. Paris, France

B. Sydney, Australia

C. New York, New York

D. Tokyo, Japan

Answer Key

Which of the following is NOT a type of paint?

Answer: B. Acetone is not a type of paint and is often used for stripping or thinning paint for removal.

Which artist was born in 1853?

Answer: C. Vincent van Gogh was born on March 30, 1853; Pollock was born in 1912; Picasso in 1881; and Rembrandt in 1606.

Who painted the ceiling of the Sistine Chapel?

Answer: B. Michelangelo is the famous artist who painted the ceiling of the Sistine Chapel.

Which of the following is NOT a shade of green?

Answer: D. Magenta is a shade of pink.

Where is the largest art museum in the world located?

Answer: A. Paris, France, is home to the largest art museum in the world, The Louvre.

Activities

Research suggests that "creativity is driven by memory (Markman, 2015)." When you're forced to develop ideas, you often have to recall past events to help you shape these new creations. Whenever you challenge yourself to step outside of your comfort zone and generate ideas, you are increasing the power of the same neural network as memory.

You don't have to be the next Picasso to know how to use a paintbrush or craft a new art piece. The only thing that is required to partake in the creative process is a willingness to open your mind to new possibilities.

Self-Portrait

Many of the greatest artists of our time, and before that, have painted a self-portrait. A self-portrait is a way for you to create a physical copy of how you interpret yourself. This activity is meant to help you pay attention to the small details you have on your face. Being able to notice all those small intricacies will make it easier for you to recognize faces around you and store those faces in your memory.

To start, select your favorite artistic medium. Do you prefer using paints? Are you someone who would rather draw with a pen or a pencil? Whichever method you like to express your creativity is the medium that you should be using for this activity.

Next, you'll want to set up a mirror in front of where you will be painting or drawing. Now, take a moment to really study your face. Where are your eyes placed? What does your nose look like? How is your mouth situated on your face? Do you have any small details like wrinkles, moles, freckles, or scars? Do you have birthmarks or any other unique details on your face? How does your hair frame your face? How is your jaw situated? What is a normal facial expression for you? Do you often have a smile on your face, or are you more stern and stoic?

Once you've studied your face, it's time to start drawing your face. Start by creating the outline. This would be the shape of your face and your neck. You might even consider drawing your shoulders. However, if you would rather just stick to your face, that is also fine. Create the basic silhouette and shape. Notice any angles you have in your jaw or forehead. Do you have a very soft and round face, or do you have more detailed and strong angles to your jaw?

Now, place the big features on your face. Where are your eyes, your nose, your mouth, and your ears? Try and space these correctly based on what you see. Next, you'll want to start adding in some of the more shaded details and small intricacies that you notice. How does your nose cast a shadow on the rest of your face? How are your cheekbones placed?

Notice all these small details to help you create your portrait. Use the correct colors or paints to add even more detail, and consider creating a background as well. You can now frame this and keep this in an area that you can easily spot to serve as a reminder to check in with your face and stay mindful of small details.

You can also try this activity by creating portraits of other people! Maybe you even find an artistic partner to try this with. You can take turns drawing each other and then compare different artistic styles.

Another challenge is to redo your self-portrait in a couple of weeks or even a month. You might notice different changes over time. How do you view yourself differently later on? Is there anything that stays the same through your different self-portraits? Or do you have a completely different style the second time around? Faces are very important for our memory, so understanding how to notice all the small details of someone's facial structure will boost your ability to have long-term memory regarding facial recognition.

Random Art Challenge

The possibilities for what you can create when exploring your artistic side are endless. For that same reason, it can sometimes be hard to come up with anything at all! This next activity is a way to ensure you never struggle to come up with creative ideas. It involves creating a collection of prompts and ideas and randomly selecting them to see what you can come up with.

The supplies you will need are:

- 3 different containers, like mason jars or cans emptied and washed

- 30+ popsicle sticks

Each popsicle stick will contain a prompt. There are three different categories of prompts, including:

1. A different art medium, like colored pencils, acrylic paint, and so on.

2. Various settings, such as a bedroom, fictional setting, or place in nature.

3. A subject, like a pet, a fruit, or a tree.

Try to come up with 10 different prompts for each category. Once you've written these, place each category of prompts in a different container.

Then, when you are ready to be creative, pull one random popsicle stick from each container. Using the examples mentioned above, this might mean getting prompted to create a picture of your pet in your bedroom using colored pencils. Alternatively, you might get prompted to paint a picture of a tree in a fictional setting using acrylic paint.

Challenge yourself to create one new thing each day for a week. By the end of the week, your skills and mental abilities will be much stronger.

Below are more ideas of different prompts you can use to fill out your popsicle sticks.

Ideas for different art mediums include:

- finger painting

- colored pencils

- acrylic paints

- crayons

- oil paints

- watercolor

- ink pens

- clay

Ideas for different settings include:

- your workplace

- your backyard

- a tall mountain

- a secret valley

- a koi pond

- a museum

- a historic location

- the last place you dined out

- your neighbor's front yard

Ideas for different subjects include:

- your favorite person

- your least favorite person

- a fictional character from the last book you read

- an item you should throw away but don't want to

- a potted houseplant

- a bug

- a musical instrument

- your favorite meal

Using these examples, you might get combinations such as:

- an ink pen drawing of a bug in a historic location

- a watercolor painting of an item you should throw away but don't want to in your neighbor's front yard

- your least favorite person in your backyard using crayons

As you can see, this prompt activity will help you come up with endless creations. You can utilize this method as often as you want and keep adding more prompts to the different containers over time. The combinations are silly, unpredictable, and even inspiring! Use your creativity and let your talents flourish.

Leaf and Flower Coasters

Everyone can use an extra coaster! Keeping your home beautiful is a great way to create a warm and welcoming environment, perfect for fostering a happy and focused mindset. This activity guides you through the process of creating homemade coasters using the imprint of various leaves and flowers.

The supplies you will need are:

- clay of your choice (air drying is the easiest)

- a collection of leaves and flowers

To start, go on a nature walk or head to your personal garden if you have one. You can also use the leaves of indoor plants or silk flowers from a craft store.

Once you have your chosen foliage, roll your clay flat and smooth. Now, you can cut them into individual squares.

When you've cut your selected coaster shapes, press the petals, flowers, stems and leaves into the coasters in various patterns. To do this correctly, lightly set them face down on top of the coaster. Then, gently tap them on the surface. You can use a rolling pin, but ensure you do so very lightly so as not to change the shape of the coaster.

After you're done pressing in the shape, you can either bake them or air dry the coasters according to the instructions on the clay package.

Alternatively, you can flatten the clay, press the foliage, and then cut the shape of the coaster around the outline of the shape. This is a little more complex, however, so choose whichever method works best for you!

This activity involves multiple steps to craft something completely original. It encourages you to get out in nature while also combining your creative skills, giving your brain a full workout. You're also led to be mindful of the intricacies of a leaf's shape and outline. Not only are you strengthening your brain in the process, but you're also enhancing your home!

Paper Marbling

Abstract art is important for strengthening a mind. When art is figurative, we critique it in a different way than abstract art. Figurative art would be something like a painting of a horse. You know what you're looking at, and while there are still symbols to interpret, there is more of a structure and basis for what you're evaluating.

When looking at abstract art, our minds are inspired to be creative. You can see it as an endless amount of things. A scribbled piece of art could be an expression of one's emotions or a drawing of a map. A splattered painting could be a bustling city or a metaphorical representation of someone's chaotic thoughts.

This activity is a way to help you create your very own abstract art. Paper marbling is the process of using paint and a blank canvas to design a one-of-a-kind, unique pattern. This will challenge your brain to focus, as you only have one attempt when paper marbling. The good news is that no matter your design, you will surely have a beautiful and intricate art piece.

What you will need is:

- paper

- a shallow pan, like a cookie sheet.

- paint colors of your choice (acrylic works best)

- a towel or paper towels to dry your creation on

When you are ready, the steps are:

1. Fill the shallow pan about halfway, just enough to create a layer of water.

2. Pour small drops of your paint throughout the pan, letting it disperse through the water in a random pattern.

3. If you have them, use a toothpick to push the water around in a more intricate pattern.

4. Place your paper (or canvas of your choice) onto the surface of the water. Move it around as minimally as possible.

5. Quickly pull it up. The paint should have transferred to the surface of the paper, creating a marble design.

You can now frame it as a work of art or use it as stationary to mail a letter to a friend! The possibilities are endless. Repeat this process by using different colors, different-sized paper, and different shapes.

Memory Mosaic

Mosaics are beautiful works of art that require a creative, thoughtful process. Consider brick mosaics in walkways or glass mosaics in windows. This activity challenges you to create a mosaic of your own!

A mosaic requires different random shapes, organized to create a uniform pattern or used as a method to cover a surface. There are a few different kinds of mosaics you can make:

- Use scraps of paper cut up into different shapes to create a mosaic picture. Organize the scraps by color, then use them to create the shapes and details of your painting. Use smaller pieces to fill in the gaps so the entire picture is covered.

- Gather small stones and shells you find around your driveway or yard or on a nature walk (just don't take too many since rocks are an important part of the ecosystem!). Clean them off, and then use them to create a mosaic in the dirt in your garden. Use smaller pebbles or moss to fill in the gaps if you'd like. You will then have a long-lasting piece of art to admire!

- Collect broken or old glassware that you've been hanging onto around the house, like an old jar or cracked vase. Place these in a thick plastic bag. Using safety glasses, gloves, and crafting in a safe environment, use a hammer to break these up into smaller pieces. Then, use grout to create a mosaic with the glass on an old piece of furniture you want to spruce up.

The possibilities for mosaic creation are endless! You can create works of art and gifts for others to help explore the creative part of your brain. Any activity that requires some ideation and practical effort is one that will strengthen your cognitive abilities.

In Summary

Creativity helps you come up with new ideas, focus on one thing at a time, and utilize critical reflection skills. Every time you create, you activate different parts of your mind and memory, strengthening cognition overall. There is no right or wrong way to be creative, and there is no singular method of expressing your artistic side. Keep trying new creative activities to help you make the most of your memory.

Chapter 6:

Physical Activities to Connect the Mind and Body

Memory improvement doesn't only happen in the brain. Your entire body contributes to the way in which your brain functions. The mind and body are connected in an immeasurable amount of ways. By exercising and participating in physical activities, you can improve your memory.

Have you ever found yourself pacing when feeling nervous? Our emotions activate different regions of our brain. This means when you are able to calm your mind, you can calm your body, and vice versa (Bhandari, 2023). This chapter focuses on activities to help you do just that. Strengthening the relationship you have with your body will make you more mindful in the present, allowing you to increase focus and memory retention.

Trivia

Pick the correct answer below. The answers are at the end of the chapter.

How many neurons do we have in our brain?

　A. 55 million

　B. 300

　C. 80 billion

　D. 1 trillion

Where is the ulna bone located in the human body?

　A. Jaw

　B. Foot

C. Arm

D. Leg

Which of the following is not a bodily system?

A. Digestive

B. Epidermis

C. Integumentary

D. Muscular

What organ is a part of the endocrine system?

A. Liver

B. Pineal Gland

C. Spleen

D. Brachial Plexus

How long is an average adult's large intestine?

A. 60 feet

B. 12 inches

C. 5 feet

D. 18 inches

Answer Key

How many neurons do we have in our brain?

Answer: C. 80 billion is a rough estimate of how many neurons we have in our brain.

Where is the ulna bone located in the human body?

Answer: C. Arm bones consist of the ulna, humerus, and radius.

Which of the following is not a bodily system?

Answer: B. Epidermis refers to the surface of the skin and is not a bodily system, unlike the others.

What organ is NOT a part of the endocrine system?

Answer: B. Pineal gland refers to a gland that is a part of the endocrine system.

How long is an average adult's large intestine?

Answer: C. 5 feet is the average length of an adult large intestine.

Activities

Working out your mind requires more than just thought-based activities. When you're able to intertwine the way your body works, you improve your mental abilities as well. Over time, we can lose some physical abilities that we used to have, so it's important to know your body's limits. If anything is too difficult or causes you physical pain, it's okay to stop and take a break. Take care of your body, and remember the importance of knowing your limits.

Smile at Yourself

It's always nice to catch a smile spread across someone else's face. However, studies show that your own cheery grin can provide health benefits to your body, like boosting your immune system (Spector, 2017). When you smile, even if you aren't actually feeling happy, it triggers real happiness, therefore boosting your mood. More frequent happy moods lower your mental health risk, which is a contributor to memory loss.

This activity encourages you to smile at least three times a day. Set a timer for early in the morning, after you've woken up, one in the middle of the day, and one close to the time you fall asleep. When the timer goes off, find your nearest mirror and smile at your reflection. The feeling of the smile, coupled with the sight of you actually doing it, is sure to trigger a more authentic smile after. It serves as a reminder to stay cheery and positive throughout the day.

To take this activity to the next level, pair your smile with some positive affirmations. A positive affirmation is a short, simple statement that serves to create a happier mood and a more uplifting outlook. Positive affirmations include things like:

- I am great!

- I am smart.

- I am valued.

- Today is going to be a great day.

- Everything is going to turn out right!

Take some time to create your own affirmations in your journal. Write down things others have said to you that improve your mood or phrases you use to get through the harder moments in life.

To help you encourage more smiling, try:

- smiling at strangers, you pass (don't take it too hard if they don't smile back!)

- putting signs, pictures, or reminders to smile throughout your house

- keep a handheld mirror by your bed so you can remember to smile when you wake up and before you go to bed

Try smiling now to see how it can instantly make you feel better. The more genuine of a smile you strive for, the more authentic it will feel—though an outlandish smile could add a little humor to your day!

Number Challenge

There are many things in life we have to count. We have to count how many minutes we have left before certain tasks or events. We count how many groceries we can buy in a week based on our budget. As our memories and focus fade, figuring out certain equations can be more challenging than it used to be.

Strengthening our number-related abilities is a great way to keep our calculation skills sharp! This activity is a little different than a simple math problem. It combines more physical activity to help you connect your mind to your body.

In this activity, there will be five different charts with five different prompts. The charts have numbers that will require you to count them based on the instructions of the prompt, using different fingers as well. This combines counting with coordination, giving you a brain-boosting workout to strengthen cognition.

Challenge #1:

- Using your right pointer finger, count all of the numbers in numerical order.

15	4	11	10
13	1	12	9
14	5	2	8
16	6	7	3

Challenge #2:

- Using your left thumb, count all the numbers backward, starting with 100 and ending with 10.

100	21	41	82
10	27	69	45
32	93	55	76
78	16	39	64

Challenge#3:

- Using your middle right finger, count all the even numbers in order.

53	121	32	4
85	22	3	77
17	2	28	12
18	9	1	40

Challenge #4:

- Using your left pointer finger, count every number with a **5** in numerical order.

6	10	17	55
5	35	210	98
53	65	105	25
27	64	15	50

Challenge #5:

- Using your right pinky, count the odd numbers in numerical order.

19	20	30	29
31	13	8	3
4	21	14	33
9	6	5	15

Opposite Hand

When looking to improve memory, one important thing to know about the brain is that it is split between two sides: the left and the right. The left side of the brain controls the right side of the body, and the right side of the brain controls the left side of the body. Many of our actions become automatic over time. This can lead to a more dominant side of the body.

To strengthen your brain and create new neural pathways, use the opposite hand that you're used to for certain tasks. For example, if you're right-handed, you might often use your right hand to brush your teeth without even thinking about it. Next time you brush your teeth, switch hands for an extra boost to your brain power.

Additional examples include:

- eating with the opposite hand

- writing with the opposite hand

- mixing or cooking with the opposite hand

- sleeping on the other side of the bed

- putting the opposite shoe on first that you normally do

- tying your shoes with a new knot method

- using your computer mouse with the opposite hand

- sitting in new spots in your living room that you don't normally sit in

- taking different routes home when walking or driving (so long as you don't get lost or take a risky route)

Coordination Tests

Our bodies are vessels for our mind, so knowing how to keep your coordination in check will help with your mental capacity just as much as your physical strength. For this activity, first do a quick assessment to see how well your coordination is. If you have any physical disabilities, this might be more challenging, so feel free to skip this activity and move on to the next to improve coordination without having to stand.

There are a few ways to check your coordination:

1. See how long you can stand on one foot. Use a timer to keep track, and make sure you stand close to something to keep you steady, like a sturdy piece of furniture or handrail. If you are able to stand for a few seconds, that's a great sign.

2. Stand up from any type of seating, and note how challenging this might be. If you notice your back tensing or you place your hands on your knees, you might find that it's actually harder to stand up ("Test Your Coordination," n.d.).

To keep working on your mental and physical health, focus on your coordination. Pay attention to how you sit or stand, and try to focus on reducing types of physical assistance to do so.

In addition, practice standing on one leg when you can. Don't cause unnecessary strain or pain to do so. To do this, simply lift one leg in front of you and point your toe forward. Try to increase the time you spend doing this each day, and always remember to have some sort of support close by to prevent any falls or injury.

Finger Yoga

There's a lot we can do with our hands. These powerful tools are important parts of our body to focus on strengthening. Finger yoga is a way you can stretch and work out your phalanges. By doing so, you are working out your mind while extending your cognitive functioning all the way to the tip of your fingers. Below are a few yoga moves and stretches to try:

1. Place your fingertips together, creating a sphere with your hand. Keeping your fingertips in place, slowly move your palms towards each other. As you do, you should notice your fingers becoming flat against one another until your hands are flat against each other, such as in a praying position. Slowly pull your palms away from each other, reverting back to that sphere structure. Repeat three times.

2. Make a fist with both hands. Stick out your right thumb. Next, stick out your left pinky. Count to three, and do the opposite finger movement on the other hand. This would mean sticking out your right pinky and left thumb. Keep swapping for five rounds.

3. Cross your pointer and middle fingers on both hands. Touch your right pointer finger to your left middle finger and your left pointer finger to your right middle finger. It's confusing at first, and you will have to find a comfortable position, but you will get it eventually. Relax your hands and repeat two more times.

Consistently doing these stretches can strengthen your brain, therefore boosting your memory in the process.

In Summary

Studies prove that physical activity, such as walking, can reverse neurological degradation due to age (Schaffer, 2012). Not only is working out your memory important, but remember to pay special attention to your physical activity as well. Simply walking for two hours a week is enough to reverse brain damage. Find methods of utilizing your body more when reading or doing other mind-challenging activities. By doing so, you are strengthening neural pathways and helping your memory flourish.

Chapter 7:

More Methods to Implement for Brain Power

Are you already noticing the effects of these exercises on how your brain works? It is never too late to learn something new, and there is always more room for memories in your mindset. We have unlimited brain power. We just have to know how to strengthen and properly utilize that power.

Forgetting things and losing memories is natural. It's a part of life! Sometimes, we forget things that we thought we never would, and that might simply be out of our control. However, the more effort and attention we give to our memory, the more likely we are to retain certain bits of information.

This last chapter is focused on some additional memory exercises to incorporate into your life on a long-term basis. There's no one-and-done technique to memory improvement; like exercise, it's something to regularly include in your life. Remember to utilize other brain puzzles, like crosswords, word searches, and sudoku to help power up your mind.

Trivia

Pick the correct answer below. The answers are at the end of the section.

What is the tallest mountain in the world?

    A. Mount Everest

    B. Mount Kosciuszko

    C. Mount Kilimanjaro

    D. Mount Mitchell's

Which is the biggest ocean?

    A. Indian

    B. Atlantic

    C. Arctic

    D. Pacific

How many countries are there globally?

    A. 1,023

    B. 195

    C. 77

    D. 216

How many cells do we have in our body?

    A. 200 million

    B. 30 trillion

    C. 50 billion

    D. 800 billion

How long is the Earth's circumference?

    A. 256,890 miles

    B. 89,320 miles

    C. 24,901 miles

    D. 8,791 miles

Answer Key

What is the tallest mountain in the world?

Answer: A. Mount Everest is the tallest mountain on the planet.

Which is the biggest ocean?

Answer: D. Pacific is the name of the largest ocean out of the four that were listed.

How many countries are there globally?

Answer: B. 195 is the number of global countries.

How many cells do we have in our body?

Answer: B. 30 trillion is an estimate of how many cells the average human body has.

How long is the Earth's circumference?

Answer: C. 24,901 miles is the estimated length of the Earth's circumference.

Activities

Brain training for at least 75 minutes a week has been proven to improve brain function (Legg, 2023). Split this up in 10-15 minute sessions every day, or 25-minute sessions 3 days a week. Whatever time you decide to dedicate to brain puzzles, challenges, and activities is up to you. The main focus should be on consistency and dedication to maintain your cognitive function.

Item Organization

Organizing, collecting, categorizing, and sorting things can be a great way to help improve cognitive strength. When you do this, you have to evaluate different attributes of items, like their size, shape, color, and material. Organizing and sorting are some of the first things we did as learning and developing children.

Organizing and sorting can increase our logical thinking and problem-solving skills. For this activity, grab the five items that are closest to you. Then, follow the prompts below to sort them in different ways:

- Sort them by alphabetical order based on their item name (not a brand name, so soda would be S, not the brand's name).

- Sort them by their size from smallest to largest.

- Sort them in order from heaviest to lightest.

- Sort them by the alphabetical order of the color they are.

- Sort them by oldest to newest.

- Sort them by most to least valuable.

Try this at different times and with different items to help increase the difficulty of this activity and make the most of the process.

I Spy Prompts

There's a good chance you've played the game *I Spy* as a child or even an adult. It's a great way to pass the time while calling attention to our surroundings. This simple activity involves one person providing a prompt for the other person to identify.

This next exercise is similar, only now you will be playing solo. For this activity, you are challenged to identify different items on your own using the prompts provided below.

Wherever you are right now, look around and identify an item that is:

- big

- small

- smelly

- flavored

- soft

- hard

- cold

- hot

- electronic

- timeless

- useful

- not useful

To take this to the next level, go on a scavenger hunt around your home. For each prompt below, identify one thing that correlates to each. Don't worry about grabbing or holding that item. Simply identify it and move on to the next. The prompts include finding one thing that is:

- yellow

- gifted from a friend

- many different colors

- sharp

- expensive

- priceless

- something you got for free

- not owned by you

- dangerous

- exciting

- delicious

- an item you forgot you had

- falling apart

- brand new

- dirty

- squeaky clean

- hidden from others

- filled with words

Now, take I Spy outside! Identify one thing that is:

- green

- rough

- tan

- scratchy

- aromatic

- alive

- filled with another item

- made of wood

- made out of stone

- a copy of another thing

- made out of glass

- an ugly color

- completely unique

Spelling Challenge

Words can be powerful tools for helping to strengthen our memory. For this activity, look at each word provided below. Use those letters to develop as many different words as possible. The only rule is that the word should be four letters or more. Feel free to use names, proper nouns, and cities if you can! The point of this activity is to help you break apart a word and use logical thinking skills to find alternate examples.

Additionally, use a scrap piece of paper to cut up small squares. Write each letter of the word on a scrap piece and scramble the letters to help you discover potential combinations. This will give you a more physical and visual method to find new words.

This is an activity that you can do with any word, but there are a couple of examples below to give you an idea of just how many combinations you might find.

How many words can you come up with using the letter of these words?

- house

- flower

Answer key:

House	Flower
• hose	• flew
• hues	• floe
• shoe	• flow
	• fore

House	Flower
	• fowl
	• froe
	• frow
	• lore
	• lowe
	• orle
	• role
	• rolf
	• wolf
	• wore
	• lower
	• rowel
	• flower
	• fowler
	• reflow

As you can see, even simple words have multiple combinations. Some words will have a lot, and others will only have a handful. It's up to you to find the combinations! Consider words like:

- taste

- forage

- person

- laminate

- sandwich

These words offer a variety of letters to help you discover many different potential combinations.

Use words of things around you. For example, how many combinations can you come up with for floor, rug, hand, or window? Breaking apart words and seeing letters in new ways will help you unlock your mental abilities to a new level.

Copy the Block

For this memory activity, you will study the pattern of the charts below and then try to replicate it using only your memory. This is challenging because you have to take the time to study the placement of the letter X in each chart. The instructions are as follows:

1. Grab a blank piece of paper. You can use grid paper as well.

2. Create a table that is five blocks in length and 5 blocks in width.

3. Grab a timer and set it for one minute.

4. Start the timer and study each table presented below.

5. Once the timer is up, do your best to recreate the pattern that was studied in the chart.

6. After you're finished, compare your results to the original.

7. Keep track of your score to see how well you did after finishing all 10 tables.

To calculate your score, add a point for each block you got right, including both squares that were left blank, or include an X. The highest possible score is 25. Then, multiply your score by four. That will be your percentage. If you got 25 out of 25 right, that would be a 100% score. If you only got 15 out of 25, that would be 60$.

Below is an example to help you calculate your score.

Example Original Table:

X			X	X
	X		X	X
		X	X	
X				
X	X	X		

Example Recreated Table:

X			X	X
	X	X	X	X
X				
X	X	X	X	

As you can see, the pattern is slightly different. 21 out of 25 of the squares were correctly copied. This would result in a score of 84%.

Below are some additional tips to help you make the most out of this activity:

- Look at large blocks to try and see memorable shapes.

- Scan from left to right to try and remember the repetition.

- As an alternative method, try focusing on the blank squares instead of the ones that include an X to see if this helps you remember more.

Now is the time to try this activity yourself! Return to these as needed to see if your scores improve over time:

Table #1:

X				X
				X
	X	X	X	
		X	X	
			X	

Table #2:

X		X		X
X	X			
			X	X
X		X		X

Table #3:

X				
	X	X		
			X	X
X			X	X
X	X			X

Table #4:

X		X		
		X	X	X
X	X	X		
X		X	X	
	X			X

Table #5:

		X	X	X
X	X	X		X
	X		X	X
	X	X	X	
			X	

Table #6:

	X	X	X	
		X	X	X
	X	X		X
				X

Table #7:

			X	
X	X	X		
	X			X
	X	X	X	
		X		

Table #8:

X				X
X	X			X
	X			
	X	X	X	X
X				X

Table #9:

		X	X	X
		X	X	
	X	X	X	
X				X

93

Table #10:

				X
	X			X
X	X	X	X	X
X	X			
X				

Daily Word

The last activity is actually a challenge! Your challenge is to learn a new word every day. There are a few different ways you can do this:

- Purchase a dictionary or thesaurus and a dice. Roll the dice 1-3 times each day to create a number. Use that number to turn to a page in the dictionary, and then select a random word you've never heard before. For example, if the first roll is a 1, the second roll is a 3, and the third number is a 6, turn to page 136 and find a random word.

- Download an app that provides a new word each day.

- Ask your preferred search engine for a random word until you get one you've never heard of before.

Once you've found your word, the next challenge is to use it in a sentence! Not only are you opening up your brain to new experiences by teaching it something new, but you're also providing a creative outlet and encouraging ideation.

The last part of the challenge is to use it in a conversation with someone. Use it in a text to a family member, call a friend on the phone and use it, or say it to the local barista as you thank them for your coffee!

For example, if the word of the day is: **Mellifluous**

According to Merriam-Webster, this word means: "having a smooth, rich flow ("Mellifluous," n.d.).

- A sentence to use in a journal entry might be, "The dripping of my coffee into the pot this morning was a welcomed, mellifluous noise for my groggy mind."

- Then, in person, you might ask a friend, "Have you heard of this band before? The singer's voice is mellifluous."

Challenging your brain several times a week will ensure you are always advancing your cognitive skills.

In Summary

If a problem challenges your mind, follow that issue to find a solution! If someone forces you to think in new ways, keep talking to them. If an experience inspires you to think in new ways, keep doing that same thing. Anytime your mind feels challenged is an opportunity to learn more and grow your thinking abilities. Memory retention is an ongoing process, so make it a priority going forward.

Conclusion

There's nothing more mind-opening than a good mental workout. Utilizing every part of your brain is a great way to ensure you stay sharp well into your golden years and beyond.

Memory loss can be scary at times, but it is a natural part of life. We will all lose brain cells over time, and some we will never get back. However, with the right tools and exercises, we can reverse any brain damage that's occurred to help strengthen many of our cognitive abilities.

Remember that there is no rush to move through the activities. They should be taken at a slow pace to help you make the most of them. The key to rebuilding your mental abilities is to stay consistent, so this means slow and frequent practice is much better than doing it in quick, short bursts spread far apart.

Whenever you feel your memory start slipping or struggle to recall information, take a step back and allow yourself room to reflect. The information you're looking for is in there somewhere! Don't fret when you find it hard to recall facts, faces, or other facets of your memory. Stress and anxiety can exacerbate a fading memory, so keep things tight and sharp by keeping your cool and giving your brain time to recollect.

Return to the activities over time, even after you've completed them. Repetition can help reinforce new ideas and thoughts you've learned. When it comes to creative activities and other challenges, you might find that your results drastically change with each attempt you make.

Pair these activities with other brain-boosting hobbies like reading, board games, and even just socializing. Enlisting a friend or family member's help in completing these activities will make them even more memorable.

There is always room to improve your cognitive abilities, and a dedication to your memory will have beneficial results. You will be able to strengthen your memory, even at times when it might not feel that way. Consistency is key, and most importantly, have fun!

Dear Reader,

We hope you enjoyed this memory-stimulating workbook. We would be so thankful for a review on Amazon if you have a moment. This will enable us to continue producing new creative books.

Feel free to contact us directly at the link below and let us know how we can improve our products. We read all input and use it to make positive changes.

We publish many self-help books, self-esteem workbooks, educational workbooks, adult coloring books, journals, organizers, sketchbooks, and activity books.

We encourage you to try them all!

You can find us at:

www.creativeworksbooks.com

References

Bhandari, T. (2023, April 19). *Mind-body connection is built into brain, study suggests*. Washington University School of Medicine in St. Louis. https://medicine.wustl.edu/news/mind-body-connection-is-built-into-brain-study-suggests/

Going outside-even in the cold-improves memory, attention. (2008, December 16). Michigan News. https://news.umich.edu/going-outsideeven-in-the-coldimproves-memory-attention/

History of the game. (n.d.). USA Pickleball. https://usapickleball.org/what-is-pickleball/history-of-the-game/

How to identify planets in the night sky. (2020, January 13). Adler. https://www.adlerplanetarium.org/blog/how-to-identify-planets/

Legg, T. (2023, June 20). *How to improve your memory: 8 techniques to try*. Medical News Today. https://www.medicalnewstoday.com/articles/326068

Markman, A. (2015, October 6). *Creativity is memory*. Psychology Today. https://www.psychologytoday.com/us/blog/ulterior-motives/201510/creativity-is-memory

Mellifluous. (n.d.). Merriam-Webster. https://www.merriam-webster.com/dictionary/mellifluous

Memory Loss. (n.d.). Cleveland Clinic. https://my.clevelandclinic.org/health/symptoms/11826-memory-loss#care-and-treatment

Memory loss: When to seek help. (n.d.). Mayo Clinic. https://www.mayoclinic.org/diseases-conditions/alzheimers-disease/in-depth/memory-loss/art-20046326

Memory. (n.d.). Harvard Health Publishing. https://www.health.harvard.edu/topics/memory

Memory: 5 ways to protect your brain health. (n.d.). Johns Hopkins Medicine. https://www.hopkinsmedicine.org/health/wellness-and-prevention/memory-5-ways-to-protect-your-brain-health

Numbers of insects (species and individuals). (1996). Smithsonian. https://www.si.edu/spotlight/buginfo/bugnos

Schaffer, G. (2012, August 27). *Boosting brain power through a mind-body connection*. Association for Psychological Science. https://www.psychologicalscience.org/observer/boosting-brain-power-through-a-mind-body-connection

6 simple steps to keep your mind sharp at any age. (2020, May 26). Harvard Health Publishing. https://www.health.harvard.edu/mind-and-mood/6-simple-steps-to-keep-your-mind-sharp-at-any-age

Spector, N. (2017, November 28). *Smiling can trick your brain into happiness — and boost your health.* NBC news. https://www.nbcnews.com/better/health/smiling-can-trick-your-brain-happiness-boost-your-health-ncna822591

Staying healthy to help your memory. (2021, August 11). Alzheimer's Society. https://www.alzheimers.org.uk/get-support/staying-independent/staying-healthy-help-memory

TED: The Economics Daily. (n.d.). U.S. Bureau of Labor Statistics. https://www.bls.gov/opub/ted/2022/men-spent-5-6-hours-per-day-in-leisure-and-sports-activities-women-4-9-hours-in-2021.htm

Terry-Cobo, S. (2012, August 2). *The hidden costs of hamburgers.* PBS. https://www.pbs.org/newshour/science/the-hidden-costs-of-hamburgers

Test Your Coordination. (n.d.). Art of Performance. https://www.at-performance.com/coordination-test.html

The power of creative thinking to improve your memory. (n.d.). Life Enriching. https://lec.org/blog/lifestyle/the-power-of-creative-thinking-to-improve-your-memory/

3 ways getting outside into nature helps improve your health. (2023, May 3). UC Davis Health. https://health.ucdavis.edu/blog/cultivating-health/3-ways-getting-outside-into-nature-helps-improve-your-health/2023/05

Timsit, A. (2023, January 26). *New study finds 6 ways to slow memory decline and lower dementia risk.* The Washington Post. https://www.washingtonpost.com/wellness/2023/01/26/dementia-memory-loss-lifestyle-habits/

Watson, S. (2016, August 17). *9 brain boosters to prevent memory loss.* WebMD. https://www.webmd.com/healthy-aging/features/9-brain-boosters-to-prevent-memory-loss

Why is socialization important for brain health? (n.d.). Asbury. https://www.asbury.org/blog/socialization-important-for-brain-health/

Why socialization is essential for people living with dementia. (n.d.). Seniors at Home. https://seniorsathome.jfcs.org/why-socialization-is-essential-for-people-living-with-dementia/

Williams, V. (2019, April 19). *Mayo Clinic minute: the benefits of being socially connected.* https://newsnetwork.mayoclinic.org/discussion/mayo-clinic-minute-the-benefits-of-being-socially-connected/

Image References

ELG21. (2020, May 6). *Landscape, summer, beach.* [Image]. Pixabay. https://pixabay.com/photos/landscape-summer-beach-seagulls-5137147/

Mallander, J. (2014, December 3). *Kittens, cats, lawn.* [Image]. Pixabay. https://pixabay.com/photos/kittens-cats-lawn-animals-mammals-555822/

Pexels. (2016, November 28). *Building, business, design.* [Image]. Pixabay. https://pixabay.com/photos/building-business-design-display-1867350/

Ritae. (2020, September 17). *Fruit, food, fruit plate.* [Image]. Pixabay. https://pixabay.com/photos/fruit-food-fruit-plate-bio-5578371/

Wellington, J. (2015, May 23). *Planting, herbs, nature.* [Image]. Pixabay. https://pixabay.com/photos/planting-herbs-summer-gardening-780736/

Printed in Great Britain
by Amazon